T0065636

HE CALLED
My Name

June O. Buggy

WESTBOW
PRESS
A DIVISION OF THOMAS NELSON
& ZONDERVAN

Copyright © 2022 June O. Buggy.

All rights reserved. No part of this book may be used or reproduced by any means, graphic, electronic, or mechanical, including photocopying, recording, taping or by any information storage retrieval system without the written permission of the author except in the case of brief quotations embodied in critical articles and reviews.

This book is a work of non-fiction. Unless otherwise noted, the author and the publisher make no explicit guarantees as to the accuracy of the information contained in this book and in some cases, names of people and places have been altered to protect their privacy.

The names in this book are fictional to protect the innocent. Neither were real locations used; no restaurants, hospitals, organizations, high schools, universities, or educational establishments are mentioned by their names. All identities are hidden to the best of my ability.

WestBow Press books may be ordered through booksellers or by contacting:

WestBow Press
A Division of Thomas Nelson & Zondervan
1663 Liberty Drive
Bloomington, IN 47403
www.westbowpress.com
844-714-3454

Because of the dynamic nature of the Internet, any web addresses or links contained in this book may have changed since publication and may no longer be valid. The views expressed in this work are solely those of the author and do not necessarily reflect the views of the publisher, and the publisher hereby disclaims any responsibility for them.

Any people depicted in stock imagery provided by Getty Images are models, and such images are being used for illustrative purposes only. Certain stock imagery © Getty Images.

Scripture marked (KJV) taken from the King James Version of the Bible.

Scripture quotations marked (AMP) are taken from the Amplified Bible, Copyright © 1954, 1958, 1962, 1964, 1965, 1987 by The Lockman Foundation. Used by permission.

ISBN: 978-1-6642-5956-0 (sc)
ISBN: 978-1-6642-5958-4 (e)

Library of Congress Control Number: 2022904083

Print information available on the last page.

WestBow Press rev. date: 03/09/2022

In memory of my mother, a wonderful mother and woman of God. She prayed for her children and grandchildren that God would increase our territories and save our souls. Her favorite scripture was Psalm 23 (the Lord is my shepherd). Lord, thanks for a wonderful mother and for allowing us to love her until her last day. I miss you, Madea, and I know you are in the arms of Jesus, resting and enjoying your eternal heavenly life. I will see you on the other side. Til we meet again, sweet mother.

See you in heaven!

Your daughter,

June O. Buggy

Contents

Chapter 1

The Family

The Family

When I was born, my mother named me after her stepmother, who called me her namesake. She found my middle name in a baby book. My last name was given to me by my dad's grandfather, Papa. However, dad's father, Roe, was what we called a "hit and run." Papa said he almost killed Roe because he would sneak into my grandmother's bedroom late at night. Well, he must have been successful with his sneaking, because nine months later, my dad was born.

Well, Papa refused to give my dad Roe's last name because he said my grandfather was no good. I have a vague memory of Granddaddy Roe. I don't remember him talking to me or giving me anything to eat; nor did he play with us. I never understood how a granddad could not spend time with his grandchildren. Maybe Papa would not let him see my dad. Roe refused to spend any time with us or his son. Therefore, my daddy became a Blue and not a Green, which was Roe's last name.

Papa also said Roe was a Geechee from Louisiana. He was a Geechee because he was black as tar, so Papa said. Papa had a way of describing people he did not care for. As a child, I never knew what a Geechee was. It truly did not matter to me or my siblings. I would later look up its meaning and be surprised to find that *Geechee* refers to a dialect of African origin spoken by descendants of African American slaves who settled near Georgia's Ogeechee River and to the people who spoke this dialect (*Merriam-Webster*).

As I grew up, I felt it would have been fun to have my paternal grandfather's last name, Green. Why? It seemed exotic and colorful, and in my mind, a name from a faraway place. At times, I could be a romantic, adventurous person, and even as a kid, I always dreamed of faraway places.

Life was pleasant. I remember taking naps and waking up on Grandma May Lee's bed with a cool breeze blowing in my face. I could sleep for hours in May Lee's bed. It was soothing, and there I could dream of faraway places I had never been. I was safe in Grandma May Lee's bed. At times Grandma May Lee made me feel cuddly and warm with her sweet singing voice; she sang around the house all the time. That cool breeze and her singing took me far, far away into an unknown land. It took me to the land of milk and honey, the land of promise—anywhere but a place of molestation, nightmares, and fear. I will get to that part later in my story.

We kids loved our paternal great-grandparents. See, my father's mother was thirteen years old when she delivered my dad; he always felt she was his sister instead of his mother. Grandma May Lee was too young to rear my dad, so Grandma May Lee's ma and dad raised him.

Here, I must distinguish the names of my sweet mothers. We called our great-grandmother Mama and called our mother Madea. We called dad's mother Grandma May Lee. While growing up, I always felt Grandma May Lee did not love us as she loved our cousins, but she did. I guess it is possible that, because she saw us all the time, we became a commonality to her. However, having a child's mind, it was easy to feel like Grandma May Lee did not love us like the others, who only came for family reunions.

Grandma May Lee also delivered my two aunts and the subject of this story, my relative whom I will call Stacks. I will get to that part of my life later. Grandma May Lee married a man named Styles, and to that union, Uncle Stacks and the youngest of my two aunts were conceived. My father was the eldest, and his dad was Grandma May Lee's first love encounter. Daddy's grandparents reared him, and they were very passive and lenient parents. They did not believe in spanking or what we called whooping. Papa and Mama may have given him a few licks every now and then. I know they hated to see him pout therefore, my dad got away with bad behavior.

Chapter 2

My Country Lifestyle

As far back as I can remember, life was fun, pleasant, and real. If we were poor, we never noticed. I guess being poor meant our parents kept us safe and comfortable, and money was not our primary objective at that time. Of course, we needed money, but our health and welfare were top priority. We were reared on a so-called farm, which was convenient, especially for food and exercise. Everything we ate was grown in our small garden.

As children, we loved fruit, especially plums, peaches, and apples. We discovered an orchard of plums and peach trees behind the house. Those trees seemed to have grown out of nowhere. *An orchard*, I thought. That day when we found the "orchard," we climbed the trees. And wow, those were the best fruits we had ever tasted. The apple trees were on the other side of the backyard. When Madea found them, she baked apple and peach pies.

Growing up, I was a tree climber. Madea would say she did not know how to stop me from climbing trees. Because I was a girl, she thought I should not do such things. Because she said, she had borne a girl child, not a tomboy.

Madea relayed that information to our babysitter Aunt Lissa. She told Madea to put me in a dress; she thought this was a cure, and that I would be too embarrassed to climb the trees because my brothers would see my panties. Aunt Lissa did not exactly know me. Dresses did not stop me from climbing or hanging upside down from any tree. I loved to climb. And hanging on a tree was where I thrived.

What else was there to do on this so-called farm with dilapidated duplexes?

Nevertheless, our step-granddaddy, Styles, caught us in the trees and warned us not to eat those green plums because they would give us the "flux." The flux? To this day, I do not know exactly what the flux is. Maybe he meant diarrhea? Who knows? We ate them anyway, green, or red, and never got the flux. I think he really said that to deter us from eating the peaches and plums he wanted Grandma May Lee to can for the winter.

The duplex we lived in was attached to our great-grandparents' place. The house sat on cinder blocks; dogs and snakes and scorpions would crawl under it. Madea was afraid those small critters would get in our beds, bite us, and "kill us dead." She was protective and eccentric to the point she checked our beds almost every night. Madea always said it was the worst place to live, not just because of the critters but because Daddy's grandparents would give him anything he wanted, even if they could not afford it.

Daddy was spoiled. He never got a whooping from his grandparents. At times, he seemed to beat them down with his tongue; he was terribly mean to them. I remember Papa would cry like a baby, especially when Daddy would threaten him with a nursing home as he aged. Papa had such a fear of those places he could not stand to talk about them at all. Madea said we should have lived somewhere else just so our father would grow up without his grandparents enabling him; it was a disaster.

———◆◆◆———

When it came to punishment, there was a distinction made in my family. Let me explain. Spanking was a pat on the behind. Whooping was done with an object such as a willow switch from the tree or a belt from Papa's waist. *If* Papa or Mama had whooped Daddy, they would have held one arm in the air and lit into him with the switch or belt. I think it would have hurt Papa just as much as it did Daddy—well, I am guessing. Daddy was never spanked or whooped as far as I was concerned.

Now, do not judge my family. I have lived a particularly good life. Of course, I remember my whooping's, but they were few and far between. Madea was the disciplinarian in the family. We did not wind up with mental wellness issues from a whooping. We learned to obey, love, and honor our parents because of the respect instilled by the punishments. Moreover, at times, we truly deserved them; we were what we called *bad*, and I wanted my way at any cost.

When we were in church, Madea could look at us a certain way, and it would send chills up and down our spines. She meant business, and our father did not believe in corporal punishment. He would yell at us, and we would look at our mother, wondering where that voice came from; it was unfamiliar. He was never home. He worked all the time, and when he had a break, he was deep into his nightlife.

Daddy worked and played hard. He could sing and play a guitar. Our mother told us he played at a juke joint, and all the women loved his curly locks, his slender body and dark skin, and his golden voice.

However, at times, Madea would get a sitter and go with Daddy to the juke joint or club. She did not like going but wanted to keep a hold on her husband and the father of her children. Daddy was kind of on the wild side. And he enjoyed life like other men, whether he was married or not. The marriage did not hold him back from a fun time. And a good woman should be home taking care of the family. That was her job (so he said). A double standard was a reality in our home; he was the boss, and our mother made sure we respected him regardless.

Madea did not like a worldly lifestyle; she felt the hand of God pulling on her to live a different life. Madea told me of a time she had tried to drink whiskey and her head had spun as if she was on a roller coaster; she'd also lost all the food she ate, and she never drank again. She tried smoking and was not able to fulfill that goal either. She never smoked again. In her mind, this was the working of God, who was trying to tell her something.

Daddy did not like "sanctified women," and she had better not go to his mother and stepdad's house across the way and get saved, not in his house. You see, Step-grandfather Styles and Grandma May Lee had prayer service all the time. They were both saved and sanctified, speaking with unknown tongues. An example of the practice can be found in the book of Acts 2:2 (KJV) which states, "And suddenly there came a sound from heaven, as of a rushing mighty wind, and it filled the whole house where they were sitting. Then there appeared to them cloven tongues, like as of fire, and one sat upon each of them. And they were all filled with the Holy Spirit and began to speak with other tongues, as the Spirit gave them utterance" (KJV, Nelson 2017).

This is one time Madea disobeyed Daddy. When he went out to have his fun, she was eager to go pray with the grandparents. Madea received Christ as her Lord and Savior, speaking in tongues as the Spirit gave utterance. How do I know this? I was there—a little girl watching on in unfamiliar territory. Madea wanted to take her chances. Daddy could not save her soul. She knew she had to die one day, and daddy had nothing to do with her soul. Madea was a pretty lady. She had dignity and grace about her. But she was no pushover; neither was she naive.

Daddy was at times mean-spirited, especially when he drank or came home wasted. My older brothers were teens at that time, and they tended to do what teenage boys do— search for girls and drive cars. Where we lived, they had to walk miles to find girls, or they would see them at school.

———◆•◆•◆———

Well, enough of that. I must have been about three or four years old when I noticed differences in the sexes. Sure, I had three older brothers. But as far as I was concerned, they were my brothers and protectors and nothing else. They were ten to twelve years older, except for the younger of the bunch, who was eighteen months older than me. It did not matter to me. We fought all the time. I would hit, scratch, kick, and whatever it took to hurt them. That was my aim as a younger sibling—to hurt those brothers, ha ha. That was always my intention when I fought my brothers. I was in charge.

I was an intensely scared kid; I feared everything and anything. Madea would say I was afraid of my own shadow. Later, I realized there was a reason I was afraid all the time. My imagination was out of this world. I could see monsters out of shadowy shapes, especially at night. I was scared when the wind blew; if it sounded like a howl, look out—no rest for Madea that night.

I can remember when Mama, my great-grandmother, was dying in the duplex next to us. I heard her screaming in agonizing, excruciating, dreadful pain. Madea said no one knew why she was having so much pain. Mama and Papa did not believe in going to the white doctor. They were afraid he would give them medicines that would kill them.

Daddy would always joke about the dentist, who would not give black people drugs to numb the gums but, instead, would just yank the tooth out. According to Daddy, black people would bleed almost to death and scream and holler with pain from the extraction. Until the day Daddy died, he never went to the dentist. I guess he believed his own stories. Or maybe it was true, and it frightened him. There was a lot of injustice done to blacks in his day. I always saw Daddy as a great storyteller. We loved to laugh at his stale jokes. But we found some of his narratives frightening at times (well, at least I did).

There was no such thing as cancer in our family. No one had ever heard of it. But I believe, to this day, Mama had cancer of some type. To scream like that, she had to have something eating her from the inside. It was horrible, and I could not sleep or settle my nerves for days.

However, that night when Mama gave her last holler, we were standing on the porch that connected to our duplex. It was pitch-black—so dark you could not see your hands before your face. But in my mind, I could see demons and monsters coming around the house for her. Madea had to take me inside and place me in the bed. There was no sleeping that night because the dogs were coming for me and Mama. You see that night, as my great-grandmother passed away, she said she heard dogs coming for her, and in my mind, I heard and saw them too.

Wow! What a thing for a scared child like me to understand. It was so frightening I could not sleep. My mind would not stop the mania. How could I end this? I was a mess. What did great-grandmother hear? And she had said she could smell burning ash and flesh. Were burning dogs really coming to meet her? I had no recollection of dogs in heaven or hell.

I could not wait until tomorrow when the sun would be up, and I would be able to see the grass, the trees, and my family.

And was Mama really dead? I wondered. What was dead? What did dead mean?

Even now, I cannot clearly remember whether I went to her funeral; my mind will not release that information. But what I do know is Mama had to lay there all night until someone picked up her body. Who picked her up? And what did Papa do all night? I am sure he was a mess too.

If my great-grandma saw or heard something like that, I can only imagine what she endured. It is indescribable and a sight that would make you want to run for your life.

I have never read in scriptures that there are dogs in hell. However, the bible does mention 'worms' in hell. St. Mark 9:48, speaks of worms, "Where their worm dieth not, and the fire is not quenched" (KJV). Based on this verse, the Jews saws worms, and fire represented both internal and external pain; nothing could be worse. Isaiah 66: 24 describes the same fate for the sinners and the disobedient: "For the worm shall not die, neither shall their fire be quenched; and they shall be an abhorring unto all flesh" (KJV).

King Herod died a horrible death with intense pain. The Bible says he was eaten by worms from the inside out. This was seen as a type of punishment; to be eaten by worms or maggots in this manner was considered a disgraceful way to die. Herod was filled with pride, and pride is a serious sin before God. In this case, God chose to punish Herod immediately. (Acts 12:20–25 tells the story of the death of Herod.)

God does not immediately punish all sin, but He will bring all to judgment (Hebrews 9:27 KJV). The Bible also indicates that judgment will come to all who do not seek repentance.

Ecclesiastes 8:11–12—says, "Because sentence against an evil work is not executed speedily, therefore the heart of the sons of men us fully set in them to do evil. Though a sinner does evil a hundred times, and his days be prolonged, yet surely, I know that it shall be well with them that fear God, which fear before him" (KJV). I cannot leave the next verse out. Verse thirteen goes on to say, "But it shall not be well with the wicked, neither shall he prolong his days, which are as shadow; because he feareth not before God" (KJV). I am not sure If Madea and Daddy took me to the funeral. I know I was a basket case.

I do hope Uncle Stacks repent of his sins and comes clean before God. Some may believe their sins are not being punished at the time of sinning. Others may believe they are safe and have not been caught. But that does not mean they will slide by the judgment seat. Most times, we Christians seems to think that God allows sinful deeds to go unpunished and feel our burdens have doubled. Let me assure you that no evil and no sins will go unpunished. God may not punish the evildoers at the time they sin, but He sees and knows their time is at hand.

I have also learned that some people think they have options when it comes to their actions and behaviors in terms of sins because they can preach, teach, or sing gospel music. Or they believe they have an escape route to heaven or that God has given them an exception because of their "righteous" (i.e. self-righteous) ways. God does not make exception for sin. We are not punished at the same time that we sin. But God will judge us all in due time. Some of us think we are slipping by, but your time is running out. The days are evil and far spent. Come in while you have time and *repent*!

Chapter 3

Chapter 3

He Called My Name!

As far as I was concerned, Stacks did not deserve to be called "Uncle." That is a title for a loving and caring person, not a perverted child molester. I believe I was five years old—I am not exactly sure my age—when I realized people can do awful things to others, even children. When Stacks "called my name," it was an omen of things to come. I was playing out in the yard with my little sister and the neighbor's kids, and my neighbor asked why he was calling me. What did he want?

At that time, my nickname was "Ree." All I heard was "Reeeee!" He elongated my name, calling me twice as if he were calling me from across another city.

As a child, I had been taught by Madea to obey my elders, so I yelled back, "What you want?" We kids were making mud pies.

"Come here for a few minutes. I want to show you something!"

"What is it?" I yelled back.

"Come here, and I will show you!"

I was not afraid. Why was I not afraid? Maybe because he was my relative and someone who Madea trusted.

So, I went into the house. He sat down on the sofa and asked me very softly to sit in his lap.

"Why?" I asked.

He was in a compromising position, and he wanted me to touch him in an unmentionable place. I did not know what to think. I was scared out of my wits. Who could I tell? Who should I tell?

Shortly, he said I would better not ever tell anyone this secret.

I ran back outside. My neighbor asked me where I had been and what had taken me so long. I said nothing—absolutely nothing.

I did not know what to think about this first encounter. I wish I could say it was last time, but it was not. One day, he drove up on his motorcycle, and as soon as, he went into the house, he came out and asked me to come in again. I went. This time, he was lying on the bed exposed. My heart started beating faster and faster. What was going to happen to me? I think I passed out. When I came to, all I know is that it was difficult for me to walk. I was uncomfortable in a disgraceful way; I felt so ashamed.

What is going on? I asked myself. *What is this? Why me?*

I was filled with questions I could not possibly answer. Why did I feel ashamed? Was this my fault? Had I caused him to violate me? I was a kid; I did not know about things like this.

As a matter of fact, there were times I cared not to remember his disgusting acts. God seemed to have given me the ability to block out what was happening to me; but the nightmares started.

However, I am thankful for the last time. I remember it vividly. Madea had to work that day, and she felt we needed a sitter. We begged her not to let Stacks watch us; we felt we were old enough to look after ourselves. Our mother did not agree. She wanted us safe. She did not know what was happening to me. If she had, he would *not* have babysat us.

Well, she called Stacks, and he came right away (of course). In my mind, I was going to fight to the death if necessary. He was not touching me anymore. My siblings were there, but I did not know where they were at that time. All I remember is that I was sitting on couch, and he was sitting on the other side. He called my name, and I screamed "No! *No!* I'm telling Madea!"

He kept trying to convince and coerce me into coming to him. I was not going to sleep or take a nap as long as he was there—it wouldn't happen this time, I guaranteed. I felt an overwhelming strength of bravery. I knew the Lord gave me that power. Stacks had taken advantage of my childhood—but not this time.

That was the last time Madea left us in Stacks' care when she had to work. Thanks be to God, my brother and I convinced her that we were old enough to look after ourselves. I often wondered why my brother asked Mom to allow us to stay on our own. Whatever the reason, he was very convincing. He told Madea he would be responsible for his two sisters and promised that we would not go outside to play until she come home. We would play games and take naps until then. Thank you, *Jesus*! Mother agreed and allowed my brother, who was eighteen-months older than me to babysit his two sisters, and we never needed Stacks again. Alleluia!

Our older brothers were working and dating. They only watched us a few times. I would have preferred my brothers instead of Stacks. Lord forgive me, but I hated that man. He only thought of his loins and not what those selfish acts did to my mental or physical state. The damage was done. I began having nightmares that were (it seemed) never-ending.

Nevertheless, he had finally called my name for the last time, and I do not remember seeing him again until my adult life.

Chapter 4

Nightmares

My nightmares had begun to grip my nights as a part of my young life. It did not matter the issues I encountered as a child; the nightmares were inevitable. However, they did not begin until after my encounters with Stacks.

What does a five-year-old think about? Certainly not having sex with a relative—yuck—or any type of sexual relationship, for that matter. I never had any nightmares before this happened to me. I was an average child. I loved to play (as all children do).

How can an uncle molest his niece and not care how he affected her? He only wanted to feel gratification, and the result was my deep inner demons that caused my mother to want to take me to a psychiatrist?

My family did not believe in "mind doctors" (as they would say). They barely believed in any medical doctors—unless he was trusted by a previously family visit.

Stacks was a trusted family member who stole my innocence. He was immoral and selfish and a corrupt individual. Love does not destroy a loved one. I often ask myself *why* he had chosen to destroy my innocence. Maybe he was just a pervert spreading his demons. Or maybe he had been violated.

This is usually how it works. When a member of the family is molested, he or she will grow up to hurt others in the family. In *Eternal Victim, Eternal Victor*, Donnie McClurkin wrote, "A seed had been planted ... A seed of homosexuality that would be my lot to struggle with for many years to come" (McClurkin, 2001, p. 34). Donnie's molester was his uncle, and he was an eight-year-old boy. My molester was my uncle also, but the difference is I am a female.

Thanks be to God my heavenly father! I could have become anything other than what God would have me become—a child molester or a female with an enormous sexual appetite.

Demonic spirits will bring all types of spirits with them. In the Luke 8:30, "Jesus asked him, saying, 'What is your name?' And he said, 'Legion,' because many demons had entered him" (KJV). Many means many—all types of evil spirits in various shapes, forms, and fashions. After the molestation, a seed is planted, and one's sexual tendency can become whatever you yield to because a corrupt seed has been planted.

1started hearing voices and noises, and I did not understand why. I did not understand what was going on with me. I could not sleep at night. My life was on a downward spiral. But why? I felt like I lived in a bubble within myself. I was all alone and frightened and was hearing voices from another world.

What had I done to *deserve* this?!

It truly makes me angry to realize a relative had destroyed my life, spreading his demonic seeds. My mother stopped taking me to funerals because I would react horribly. I would cry and hold Daddy's neck so tightly my arms would become numb. I remember Madea saying she did not know what to do with me and that she wouldn't take me to anymore funerals. In my little mind, that dead person was going to sit up and scare me. Or he or she would come in my room that night just to frighten me.

Even when mother took us to church on the first Sunday, it was scary. You may ask why first Sunday? Well, first Sunday in Black churches represents Communion. Taken from the Bible, Communion is done to commemorate the Lord's death, burial, and resurrection and the Lord's last supper. In I Corinthians 11:23–25, where Jesus took bread and when he had given thanks, he broke it, and said, "Take eat this is my body, which is broken for you: this do in remembrance of me" (KJV).

What scared me was that the table sitting on the altar was covered with a white cloth, and something was under it. In my mind, there was a severed head under the tablecloth.

Wow! My imagination was wild. My mind would give me evil visions and sounds. This became more than I could bear. Lord, help me!

I am *not* expecting every single reader to believe my story, and it may be unbelievable to some. But it is my story. This is what truly happened. I have always tried to make sense of it. And with God's help, I will try to help others overcome some of the grim aspects of molestation.

One of my nightmares

My little sister and I slept in the same bed, which was not far from Madea and Daddy's bed. Only a curtain divided the two rooms, serving as a doorway. No lights were left on at night. We had coal oil lamps, and Madea did not burn those at night unless someone was reading. We would use the lamps as lights during dinnertime, but after that, they were put out. Therefore, there were no lights on in the house after we fell asleep.

Nighttime in the country was pitch-black—the darkest of dark nights. There was a thickness about nighttime, and I was afraid all the time.

One night as I dozed off to sleep, I heard a heavy door close. It sounded like the door to a huge bank vault. In my mind, it was as wide as the heavens and as thick as the earth. The sound was so loud in my brain it shook me to my little core. I was shaking like a bowl of jelly. I could not scream or holler. No sound would come from my mouth. I could not move.

Oh no, I cried silently. *What is it?*

I heard something growling, and I felt an animal pulling my covers off me. *No. No. Help me*, I pleaded in my mind, unable to make a sound. I could not move, and I could not holler. I remember crying and calling for my mother, but no sound came out of my mouth. If I could only move, I would run to Madea. I knew I would be safe if I could get to her. But I could not move.

Whatever had come for me kept scratching and growling as if on a mission, scratching and then gnawing at me. And still, I could not move. I needed to run and hide somewhere. But where? I searched my mind. There was no place to hide. *No, no*, I kept silently repeating. *Madea! Help me.*

It stopped as quickly as it had come for me. But why? What had caused it to stop? Or who had frightened that animal away? I then heard that huge, heavy door slam shut, and the evil spirit was gone.

When I finally was able to move, I ran out of my bed so quickly I left my nightgown behind. I jumped between Madea and Daddy. Daddy did not wake up, and Madea was scared because I was frightened. "What is the matter?" she asked.

I was shaking so much I couldn't stop. I was crying. I was scared. I had a bad dream, but it was so dark in the house I could see faces of demons. I said, "I see a face."

Mother was using the "slop jar" (some people called it that instead of toilet, but we called it a "pot") when I said that. She shot to her feet. She was frightened too. Madea said she had to do something for me. My fear was too much, and I might die from fright. She truly worried about me. But my mother was a praying woman of God.

Demons are destructive creatures of their ruler Satan, who is like a roaring lion. I Peter 5: 8 reads, "Be sober, be vigilant; because your adversary the devil walks about like a roaring lion, seeking whom he may devour" (KJV). Satan wanted to kill me, take me out, or make my life a living delusion. Satan is the master of creating suffering, despair, distractions, and manipulation.

But God said, "No!" Praise his mighty name! I did not want to live under the grips of Satan's power.

Madea took us to church. Now, for those who do not believe in God or his power, He is real. He saved me and set me free from the bondage of molestation and despair. I was free from this psychologically tormenting grip. I never had another nightmare again. Nor did I hear anymore voices. I was truly, absolutely free. I do not remember every single detail of my experience, but I remember enough to draft this book.

Madea did not stop there. She took us to Sunday school. We learned about the Lord and His saving grace and mercy. God loves me, and He freed me! I felt as if life took on a new meaning. It was all fresh and clear. I no longer lived in a deep darkness. I was free.

Satan became a defeated foe in my life. I still pray and fast for my strength and mental state. I am not saying I have mental issues. I am saying we should never stop praying because Satan is always looking for new avenues to take Christians out. Jesus told Simon Peter in Luke 22:31–32, "Simon, Simon! Behold Satan hath desired to have you, that he may sift you as wheat. But I have prayed for thee, that thy faith fails not; and when thou art converted strengthen thy brethren." (KJV).

Satan wanted to sift me as wheat too. But when my mother did not know what to do, she knew how to pray. Satan wanted to take me out through my mind and dreams. I was constantly afraid and mean to others. I always wanted to fight, and I did not take anything from anyone. I was not at rest or at peace with myself. My life was out of control. At such an immature age, where was I to go from here? I had no direction after being molested.

Chapter 5

Chapter 5

In Those Days

During those days and years when I was reared no one told or "snitched" on a relative. Relatives seemed untouchable. And besides, who would have believed me, a young child with a wild and vivid imagination?

For example, I read a story about a young girl who was raped by her first cousin. The mother caught him on top of her. When the mother told her parents, the children's grandparents, they refused to believe her. So, the mother called the police department, and the cousin was sent to a treatment center. The girl and her family were ostracized by their family. Why? No one could believe that it had happened, and the cousin said he fell on her. The family said the girl was overreacting and that she was a fast and forward individual. She was only a young girl and like any child only wanted a safe environment (Robinson and Scott 2019, 54–55).

In my case, my mother never knew what was going on with me. My abuser forced me to keep silent, and I did not know how to tell her. I felt I was the cause of this abuse. Why? I did not know. What had I done to deserve this? I never spoke about my encounters until I was twenty-eight years old, married, and had my two daughters. My nightmares were gone. Or at least they were not demonic anymore. But I still had dreams that told me of my destiny. I also do not remember telling my first husband. I was not able to share at the time.

However, I noticed how protective I was of my two daughters. I would not allow them to spend nights at their friends' houses, especially if I had not met the mothers or fathers. If a friend's mother had a spouse or brothers, they could not spend the night. I had to be sure they were safe; I was responsible for their well-being. I could not live with myself if I thought they were molested like me. I am not saying I was perfect, but I was precautious and cared where they were going. My aim was for my daughters to be free from all predators.

They were mad a few times. But pleasing them did not outweigh my desire to keep them safe. Their safety and well-being was my top priority. I knew from experience that predators are sitting next to you in church waiting for a mother to turn her back or lurking in the parking lots and groceries stores. But I was a lioness. I would not allow my children to be harmed. I knew where my children were and what they were doing. I made sure they were with my mother if they weren't with me. *All* parents are responsible for their children.

The fact that my mother did not know what was happening to me does not mean my mother didn't love me. I knew my mother loved me. There was no doubt in my mind she was very protective of me and my sister. Stacks was the only family member available, and she trusted him to watch us while she worked. Besides, he threatened me, and I was too afraid to tell. What would I say? Would she believe me? At that early age, I did not understand what the repercussions would be for me if I came forward. Nor could I know whether he would be punished for his behavior. I truly doubt that Stacks would have been punished. That is another day for another book—one that focuses on research on perverted relatives who are child molesters.

However, I am thankful that I am free from this demon of fear and that I'm no longer a child. A child is vulnerable, weak, and unable to defend him or herself, and perpetrators knows this. The enemy will attack you in your weakest areas. You must know your weaknesses, and this requires a humble heart. As a child, you do not know your weaknesses. Children are born weak, and children's innocence is openly shown to all.

As an adult, I often feel the urge to help others in distress and those who are weary because of trauma and incestuous affairs. This is because these types of traumas in one's life will lead to a downward tunnel and a disparaging life with anguish, unrest, the feeling of unworthiness, degradation, and despair. When we live with family who may not understand what we are going through, it's difficult to make others understand your dilemma without revealing the entire truth.

Remember: when one is molested, there are spirits that come within the territory, and the spirits do not come alone. They bring other spirits to torment you. They want to kill, steal, and destroy your entire life. When the seeds of sin and molestation have been planted, they germinate, root, sprout, and grow into a full-grown plant. And when others eat from it, they also become consumed.

According to researcher Yvonne Dolan, some other symptoms and challenges are the results of the survivor's spiritual wounds and mental illness. These include sleep disturbances, dissociative responses, flashbacks, concentration difficulties, memory problems, sexual dysfunction, eating disorder, self-destructive behavior, self-mutilation, depression, negative perception of self and others, and a likelihood of attempted suicide (Dolan 1991, p. 5, cited by Wisdo 2018, p.3).

In St. Matthews we read, "But when the unclean spirit has gone out of a man, it roams through dry (arid) places in search of rest, but it does not find it. When an unclean spirit comes out of a man … then it says I will return to my house from which I came. And when it arrives, it finds the place unoccupied, swept, and put in order" (St. Matthews 12:43–45 AMP). Then it goes and brings with it seven other spirits more wicked than itself, and they go in and make their home there (Matthew 12 Amplified Bible). And the last condition of that man becomes worse than the first. So will it also be with this wicked generation (*Today's Parallel Bible* 2000).

As you see, evil spirits brings others to torment you. Demons will steal, kill, and destroy. Demons have no remorse or feelings for individuals. Therefore, we as Christians must arm ourselves against the evil works of Satan. In Ephesians 6:10–13, Apostle Paul revealed to the church in Ephesus, "Finally, my brethren, be strong in the Lord, and in the power of His might. Put on the whole armor of God, that ye may be able to stand against the wiles of the devil" (KJV).

These verses were designed to encourage God's people to stand against Satan's tactics and his arrows. They are tricky, Satan and his imps. They gain power and thrive in people who are in authority—for example, your preacher, your teacher, your family members, and anyone who is supposed to watch over you. In my case, it was a relative who my mother trusted; he was a pedophile in every sense of the word.

Child sexual abuse affects not only your mind but also your soul. It is a painstaking disease that torments you day and night. You may ask yourself, how did I overcome this disease, this trauma, this infection? It was by the grace of God I was saved and by calling on His son Jesus. If not, I would have been a living mess.

Thank God for my mother and her spiritual insight. I could not have continued to live in peace without the power of the Holy Spirit. The Holy Spirit helped by revealing His magnificent power and bringing spiritual insight into my life. Now, I must maintain my spiritual needs by praying, reading the Word, fasting, and sharping my spiritual tools.

Satan has more tricks than a hound dog has fleas. I must stay spiritually sharp because times are hard, and there are all types of spirits to fight. Do not get complacent. Satan wants to catch you with your guard down. Remain vigilant. 1 Peter 5:8 says, "Be sober, be vigilant, because your adversary the devil, as a roaring lion, walking about, seeking whom he may devour" (KJV). However, I had to learn how to resist the devil—as verse nine says, "Resist him, be steadfast in the faith, knowing that the same sufferings are experienced by your brotherhood in the world" (KJV).

That is one thing about Satan. He is vigilant. He respects no one and wants to destroy everyone, especially leaders. Why leaders? Leaders have followers, and when leaders falls, others fall with them. You see, there are individuals who totally trust and believe in the leader. They do not pray unless the leader says to and so forth.

Jesus Christ saved you. Remember that your leader needs saving too. Do not give your *total* commitment to *any* man. Keep in mind that I said *total* commitment. We all must trust someone. But man will fail you. Man will deceive you. But Jesus has never failed. His track record is invincible, meaning He is incapable of being conquered, overcome, or subdued. He will not lie to you, trick you, or violate you. He will not leave you or forsake you. *He is God!* Why not serve a God like that? He is worthy of being served.

I remember placing my trust in others only to be betrayed. I worked for a company where I nearly worked myself to death. I was on time, and I put my employer first, even above my children and family. If I were sick, I would go in anyway. Even when my children were ill, if I called in, my supervisors would have disgust in their voices. I would find a sitter, just to go in and worry all day about them.

Some years later, my husband became ill and was diagnosed with cancer. I had to take a leave of absence. When I returned after two months, I was moved to another department and forced to drive to other offices at my age to cover for managers. After that, I felt the urge to retire early.

The upper management did not appreciate me. They only needed the work done under any circumstances. I wanted to lash out. But on the other hand, I understood this was my time to move on. Nevertheless, their day was coming too. We all will reap what we have sown in this life. It was unfair how I was treated, but I am happy now, and God gets the praise every day. I am doing what I desire to do.

Overall, my life as a child was not hard except when I was violated. If it were not for that awful experience, my life would have been as perfect as perfect could be. We were not rich, but life was great. We did not worry about being naked or hungry. Madea and Daddy saw to that. And in my eyes, that is perfect.

I did not like the nightmares I had. Nor, to this day, has Stacks apologized for the way he treated me. Do I expect him to? I really do think he knows how to say the words "I apologize." In my opinion, he had an opportunity to do so at his father's funeral. He seemed to have only been thinking about himself.

Style's funeral was the last time I saw him. That day, he walked up to me at the funeral with a despicable grin on his face, as if he were up to his old tricks again. God gave me the opportunity to avenge myself. I told him, if he took one more step toward me, I would kick him where the sun does not shine. He laughed and walked away. I was stronger than that little child he had taken advantage of years ago. That little child whose name he had called was no longer afraid. I faced my fears and felt like a new person.

Maybe you have not had the chance to face your fears. But pray and ask God for the opportunity to do so. Do not allow hate to build a nest in your heart. Get rid of anger and vile hatred; cleave to the Word of God. Hate only hurts you. It will tear you down. Lose it now!

Chapter 6

What Does the Bible Say about Child Sexual Abuse?

I discovered on Got Questions, a website that answers questions about the Bible, that sexual abuse perpetrated against a child is the deplorable reality of living in a sin-stricken world. The site notes, too, that the psychological, emotional, and physical damage of the abuse remains long after molestation has taken place. The Bible speaks vehemently against sexually hurting children and sexual perversion of any kind. In addition, the Bible offers hope, healing, and forgiveness for the perpetrator and the victims (2020, p.1).

Why does child sexual abuse happen?

Sometimes, hurt people hurt people, and we live in a world marred by sin. Often when others have molested children, they have been molested themselves. Some people may not have been molested, but they may have been hurt in other ways. Sexual abuse can be the result of anger, selfish ambition, or narcissism. Or it can be a misguided attempt to find intimacy (*Got Questions* 2020, 1). However, it is never—I repeat, it is never—the fault of the abused child, and the child cannot and should not be held responsible for the perpetrator's actions.

As the Bible says, caring for children in need pleases God. "Pure and undefiled before God and the Father is this: to visit the orphans and widows in their troubles, and to keep oneself unspotted from the world" (James 1:27 KJV; Vines 2018, 1,804). The Bible also warns fathers not to provoke their children to wrath but to bring them up in the training and admonition of the Lord (Ephesians 6:4 KJV). Children were always important to Jesus, and he never abused them.

He showed children love. In Matthews 19:14, Jesus said, "Suffer little children, and forbid them not, to come unto me: for of such is the kingdom of heaven" (KJV). Jesus is our prime example, and if children were important to Him, they should be important to us also.

Wherefore, I praise the living Savior for His saving grace, which brought me this far. I hope and pray that this book will bring some comfort to a dying soul, whether male or female, who has been violated by a relative or friend. God has a plan for your life. Do not give up. Look to the hills from whence comes your help. My help cometh from the Lord, which made heaven and the earth (Psalms 121:1–2 KJV).

The only reason I did not go to a therapist is my family did not believe in therapy. There is nothing wrong with going to a Christian counselor. Jesus is a counselor, a mighty God. He is a mind regulator. I had to learn to put all my trust in the Lord. I read my Bible often, and I memorized some scriptures to uplift me, and I mingled with people who had and have my best interests in mind.

I hope I have written something that will help someone's life and that you can pass this material on to others. Thank you for purchasing my book. I pray God's blessings upon your life. Yes you, I am speaking to you. Lift your head up; life is worth living with Jesus Christ!

References

References

Got Questions (website). 2020. *Questions of the Day.* Accessed December 29, 2020. https://www.gotquestions.org/sexual-abuse.html.

Hindson, E. 2017. *The King James Study Bible.* Nashville: HarperCollins Christians, Inc. Accessed August 18, 2020.

McClurkin, D. 2001. *Eternal Victim, Eternal Victor.* Lanham: Pneuma Life Publishing, Inc.

Nelson, T. 2017. *The King James Study Bible.* Nashville: Thomas Nelson. Accessed November 1, 2021.

Robinson, B., and L. C. Scott. 2019. *Protecting Your Child from Predators.* Bloomington: Bethany House.

Today's Parallel Bible. (2000). Grand Rapids: Zondervan Corp. Retrieved October 29, 2021

Vines, P. 2018. *The Vines Expository Bible.* NKJV edition. Nashville: Thomas Nelson.

Merriam-Webster, s.v. "Geeche." *www.merriam-webster.com/dictionary/Geechee.*

Printed in the United States
by Baker & Taylor Publisher Services

Printed in the United States
by Baker & Taylor Publisher Services